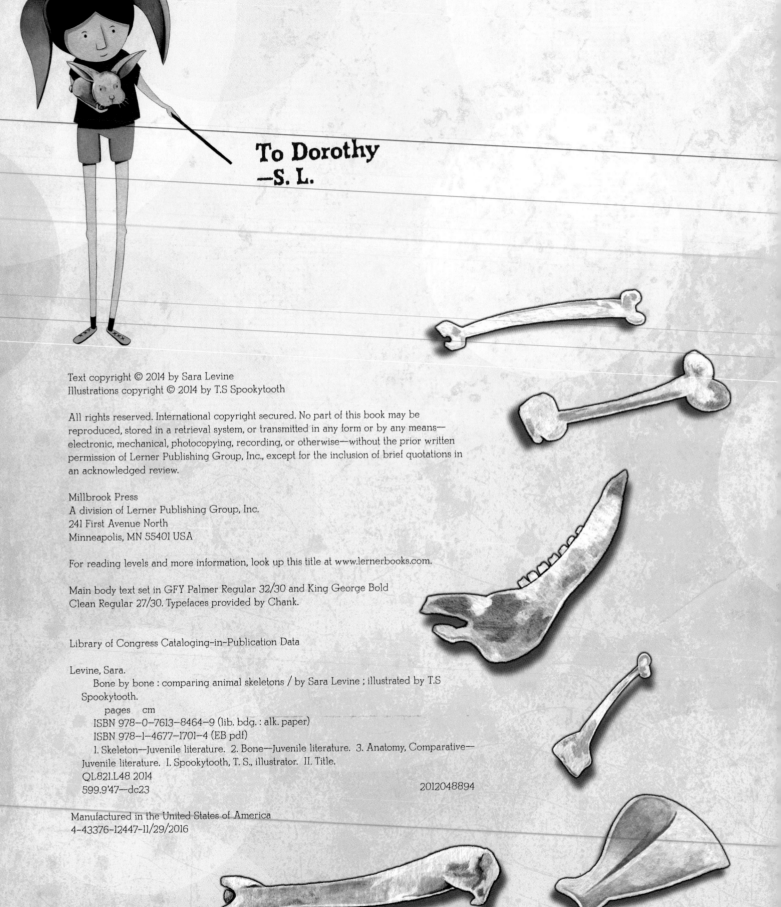

To Dorothy
—S. L.

Text copyright © 2014 by Sara Levine
Illustrations copyright © 2014 by T.S Spookytooth

Millbrook Press
A division of Lerner Publishing Group, Inc.
241 First Avenue North
Minneapolis, MN 55401 USA

For reading levels and more information, look up this title at www.lernerbooks.com.

Main body text set in GFY Palmer Regular 32/30 and King George Bold Clean Regular 27/30. Typefaces provided by Chank.

Library of Congress Cataloging-in-Publication Data

Levine, Sara.
    Bone by bone : comparing animal skeletons / by Sara Levine ; illustrated by T.S Spookytooth.
       pages   cm
    ISBN 978–0–7613–8464–9 (lib. bdg. : alk. paper)
    ISBN 978–1–4677–1701–4 (EB pdf)
    1. Skeleton—Juvenile literature. 2. Bone—Juvenile literature. 3. Anatomy, Comparative—Juvenile literature. I. Spookytooth, T. S., illustrator. II. Title.
QL821.L48 2014
599.9'47—dc23   2012048894

Manufactured in the United States of America
4–43376–12447–11/29/2016

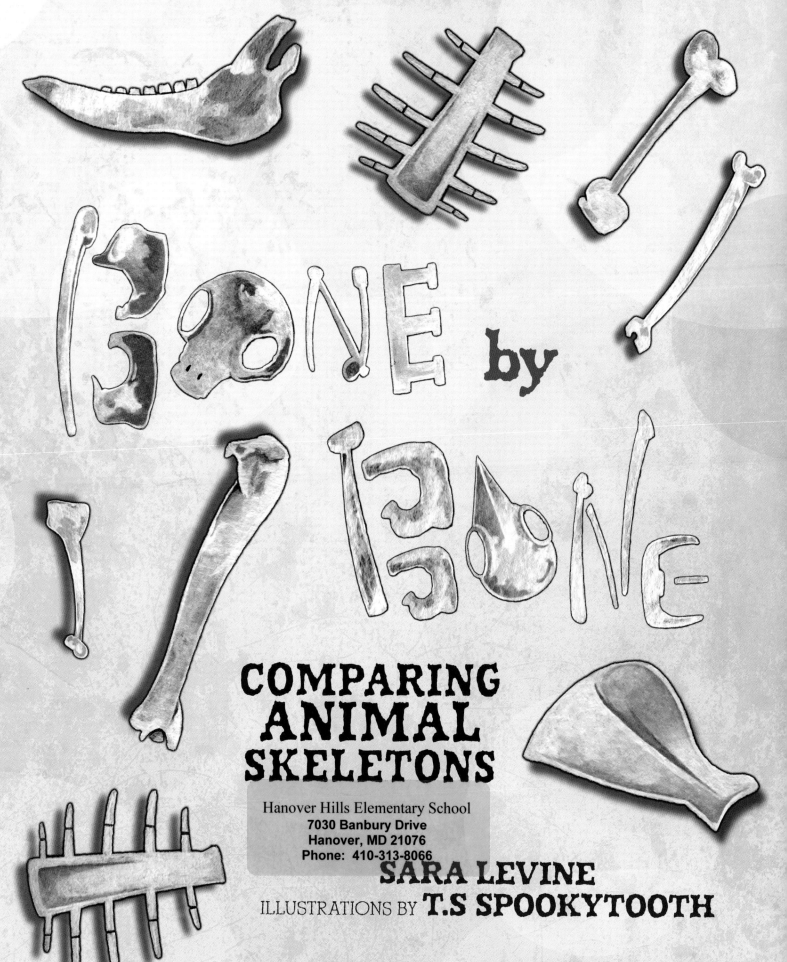

BONE by BONE

COMPARING ANIMAL SKELETONS

SARA LEVINE

ILLUSTRATIONS BY T.S SPOOKYTOOTH

M Millbrook Press Minneapolis

Have you ever wondered what we would look like if we didn't have any bones?

It wouldn't be pretty.

Luckily, we don't have that problem.
We're **vertebrates**, animals with bones.
Our bones hold us up.

Vertebrates come in different shapes and sizes, but we have many of the same bones. All vertebrates have skulls and ribs. And we all have vertebrae. Vertebrae stack up one on top of another to make the spine, or backbone.

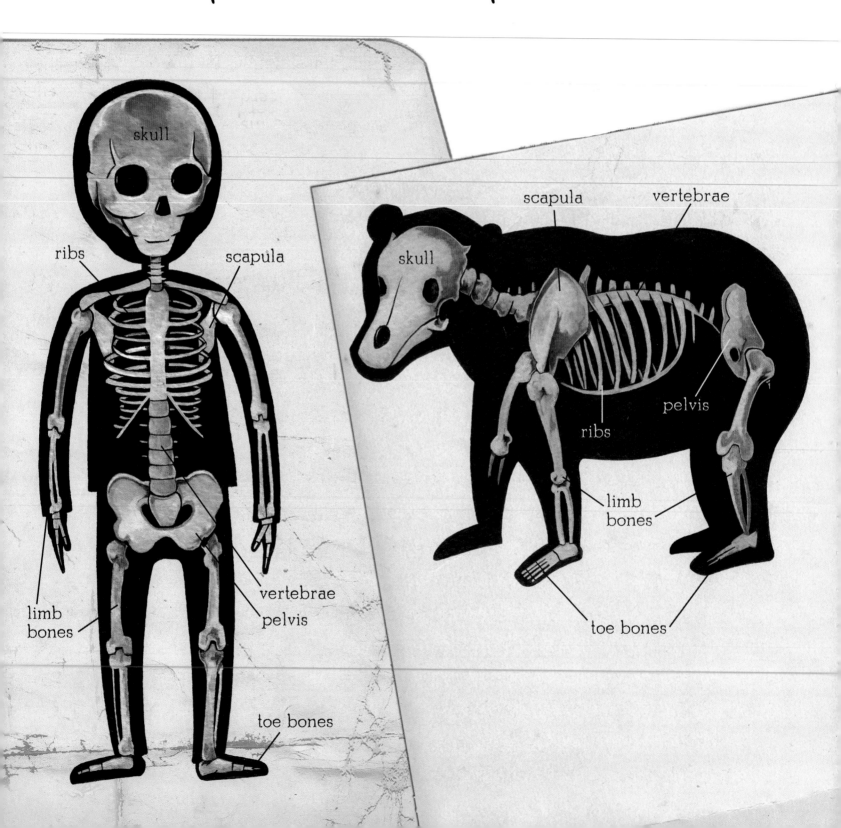

Can you imagine how you'd look if we added some bones to your spine?

What if your vertebrae didn't stop at your rear end?

What if they kept going?

YOU'D HAVE A TAIL!

Tails are made of vertebrae. Lots of animals have tails. They wag on happy dogs and sweep side to side to help alligators swim through the water.

What would happen
if we took away
some bones?

What if you
didn't have any
arm or leg bones?

What kind of animal
would you be if you had
just a skull, vertebrae, and ribs?

A SNAKE!

Snakes don't have arm or leg bones
because they don't have any arms or legs.

What kind of an animal would you be if we took away your leg bones but kept your arm bones?

Here's a hint: we'd also move your breathing holes from the front of your face to the top of your skull.

A WHALE OR A DOLPHIN!*

These animals don't have legs. Their arm bones and finger bones are flippers.

The holes on the top of their skulls are their blowholes. Blowholes let them breathe air easily as they swim.

*A porpoise is another correct answer.

Instead of tilting their heads at the surface to get air as we do when we swim, they just rise up to take a breath.

What would happen if your middle fingers and middle toes were so thick that they supported your whole body?

What kind of animal would you be if those bones were so strong that you didn't need any other hand or foot bones?

A HORSE OR A DONKEY OR A ZEBRA!

These animals have only one toe on each leg. Instead of fingernails and toenails, they have hooves.

What kind of animal would you be if you had only two fingers on each hand and two toes on each foot?

A GOAT OR A SHEEP OR A MOOSE OR A DEER OR A PIG OR A COW! *

Since these animals walk on two toenails, their hooves are called split hooves.

fig. 1

fig. 2

fig. 3

fig. 4

fig. 5

*A camel, a giraffe, and an antelope are also correct answers.

Now let's keep all of your bones but change the size of some of them.

What kind of animal would you be if you had really big vertebrae in your neck?

A GIRAFFE!

Both humans and giraffes have seven vertebrae in their necks, but giraffe vertebrae are enormous! Each vertebra can be more than 10 inches (25 centimeters) long.

That's about as big as your head!

What kind of animal would you be if your leg bones were much, much longer than your arm bones?

A RABBIT OR A KANGAROO!*

These animals need strong hind leg bones for jumping.

*A hare and a pika are also correct answers.

What kind of animal would you be if your finger bones grew so long that they **reached your feet?**

A BAT!

Bats' wings are made of finger bones. A web of skin connects the bones to make wings so that a bat can fly.

What if we took away **all** of your bones?

Could you be an animal if you didn't have any bones at all?

YES! Many animals don't have bones. They're called **invertebrates**.

Clams, beetles, and starfish have no bones. They have their hard parts on the outside.

Worms and slugs don't have bones. Their bodies are small and mushy.

Jellyfish don't have bones either. In fact, their bodies are so fragile, they would collapse if they didn't live in water.

But let's add the bones back in one more time.

What kind of animal would you be
if you could turn this page?

A HUMAN!

The bones in our hands look a lot like the bones many other animals have. But we can move our thumbs in a special way that allows us to do many things, including turning the pages of a book. Our special thumbs are called opposable thumbs.

Opposable thumbs are one of the things that make us human.*

*Apes and some monkeys have opposable thumbs too.

MORE ABOUT BONES

Bones are important because they hold us up. But they have other important jobs too.

Did you know that bones are also factories? Inside our bones is where we make blood cells.

Bones are storage areas as well. Inside our bones, we store fat and minerals for when our bodies need them.

Bones make us able to move. They can do this with help from our muscles.

MORE ABOUT VERTEBRATES

There are five different types of vertebrates: birds, mammals, amphibians, reptiles and fish. But how do we tell them apart?

Does it have feathers?
If it does, it's a bird.

Does it have hair or fur?
Does the mother make milk for her babies?
If so, then it's a mammal.

Does it have slimy skin that it breathes through?
Does it lay jellylike eggs that will dry out if they aren't in the water or under a damp log?
If so, it's an amphibian.

Does it have scaly skin?
Are the shells of the eggs hard so they don't dry out in the sun?
If so, it's a reptile.

Does it have fins and scales?
Does it spend all of its life in the water?
If so, it's a fish.

GLOSSARY

blowhole: a hole, or a nostril, at the top of a skull that dolphins, whales, and porpoises use for breathing. This hole lets them raise their bodies up to take a breath instead of tilting their heads up to the water's surface each time they need air.

flippers: the paddlelike body parts on animals that live in the water. Flippers are made of the same bones that form arms and legs on other animals, but they are shaped better for swimming.

hooves: thickened toenails at the end of the toe bones that animals walk on

invertebrates: animals without bones, including jellyfish, insects, crabs, snails, starfish, earthworms, and sponges

minerals: chemical substances in certain foods that are important for health

opposable thumbs: thumbs that can be moved so they can touch all the fingers on the same hand

ribs: the long, slender, curving bones that start at the spine and wrap around to attach to the breastbone (sternum), protecting the soft organs in the chest of an animal

skull: the bones that surround and protect the brain

spine: the stack of small bones called vertebrae that runs up the middle of the back. The spine protects the spinal cord, a large group of nerves that carries messages between the brain and the rest of the body.

vertebrae: small bones, each with a hole in the middle like a bead. Together they stack up, one on top of the other, to form the spine.

vertebrates: animals with bones. Animals that have bones include fish, amphibians, reptiles, mammals, and birds.

FURTHER READING

Books

Arnold, Caroline. *Your Skeletal System.* Minneapolis: Lerner Publications Company, 2013.
What is a bone? How do bones help your body function? Learn about the human skeletal system in this informative book.

Cobb, Vicki. *Your Body Battles a Broken Bone.* Minneapolis: Millbrook Press, 2009.
Micrographs and illustrations take you up close to find out what happens when you break a bone and how your body helps you heal.

Jenkins, Steve. *Bones: Skeletons and How They Work.* New York: Scholastic Press, 2010.
Explore the bones of humans and other animals through detailed cut-paper collage illustrations.

Johnson, Jinny. *Skeletons: An Inside Look at Animals*. New York: Reader's Digest, 1994.
This book introduces readers to the skeletons of a variety of vertebrates and includes fascinating facts about animal bones.

Parker, Steve. *Skeleton.* New York: DK Pub., 2004.
With diagrams, photos, and illustrations, this book looks closely at the functions of bone groups, shows what makes up a bone, and draws comparisons between human and animal bones.

Websites

The Children's University of Manchester: Body and Medicines—the Skeleton
http://www.childrensuniversity.manchester.ac.uk/interactives/science/bodyandmedicine/theskeleton/
This website shows you different types of bones in the human body and explains why our skeletons are so important.

Walking with Beasts—Kids Corner
http://www.abc.net.au/beasts/playground/
Test your knowledge by playing a game in which you must solve puzzles with animal bones.

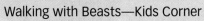

Your Bones
http://kidshealth.org/PageManager.jsp?lic=1&article_set=54029&cat_id=20607
Find out what bones are made of, how bones grow, how to take care of your bones, and more.